$16.00

To Andrew,
    Love and Godbless you
    on your Christening day &
        Bill Christl Willie and Danny

THE Story of the Creation

JANE RAY

WORDS FROM GENESIS

Dutton Children's Books • New York

For my mother and father

THE WORDS FROM GENESIS HAVE BEEN TAKEN FROM
THE KING JAMES VERSION OF THE BIBLE.

Copyright © 1992 by Jane Ray
All rights reserved. CIP Data is available.
First published in the United States 1993 by
Dutton Children's Books, a division of Penguin Books USA Inc.
375 Hudson Street, New York, New York 10014
Originally published in Great Britain 1992
by Orchard Books. Printed in Belgium.
FIRST AMERICAN EDITION
Spanish-language edition available
ISBN 0-525-44946-9

2 4 6 8 10 9 7 5 3 1

This is a story of how the world began.

And the earth was without form, and void; and darkness was upon the face of the deep.

And the Spirit of God moved upon the waters. And God said, Let there be light: and there was light.

And God saw the light, that it was good: and God divided the light from the darkness. And God called the light Day, and the darkness he called Night. And the evening and the morning were the first day.

DAY

NIGHT

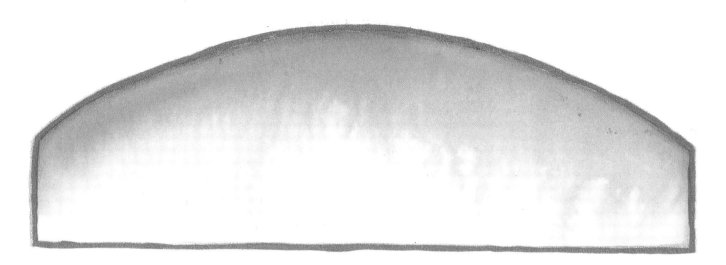

And God said, Let there be a firmament in the midst of the waters, and God made the firmament, and divided the waters. And God called the firmament Heaven. And the evening and the morning were the second day.

 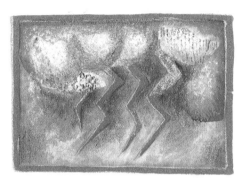 

And God said, Let the waters under the heaven be gathered together unto one place, and let the dry land appear: and it was so.

And God called the dry land Earth; and the gathering together of the waters called he Seas: and God saw that it was good.

And God said, Let the earth bring forth grass, the herb yielding seed, and the fruit tree yielding fruit after its kind upon the earth: and it was so.

And the earth brought forth grass, and herb yielding seed after its kind,
and the tree yielding fruit after its kind: and God saw that it was good.
And the evening and the morning were the third day.

MARCH   APRIL   MAY   JUNE   JULY   AUGUST

SPRING   SUMMER

And God said, Let there be lights in the firmament of the heaven to divide the day from the night; and let them be for seasons, and for days, and years. And God made two great lights; the greater light to rule the day, and the lesser light to rule the night: he made the stars also.

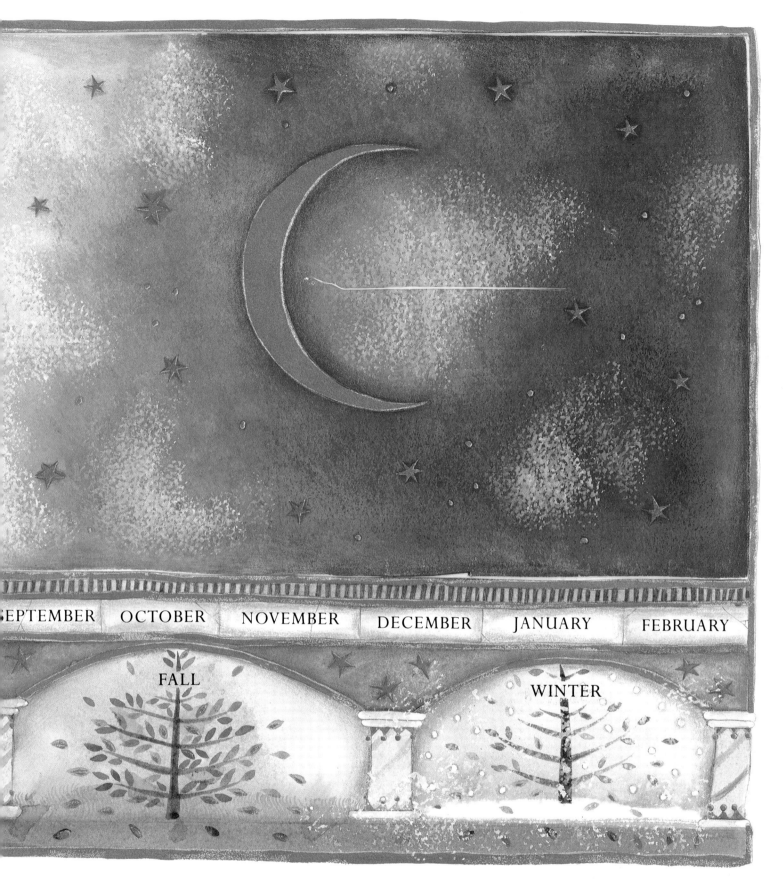

FALL

WINTER

And God set them in the firmament of the heaven to give light upon
the earth, and to rule over the day and over the night, and to divide the
light from the darkness: and God saw that it was good. And the evening
and the morning were the fourth day.

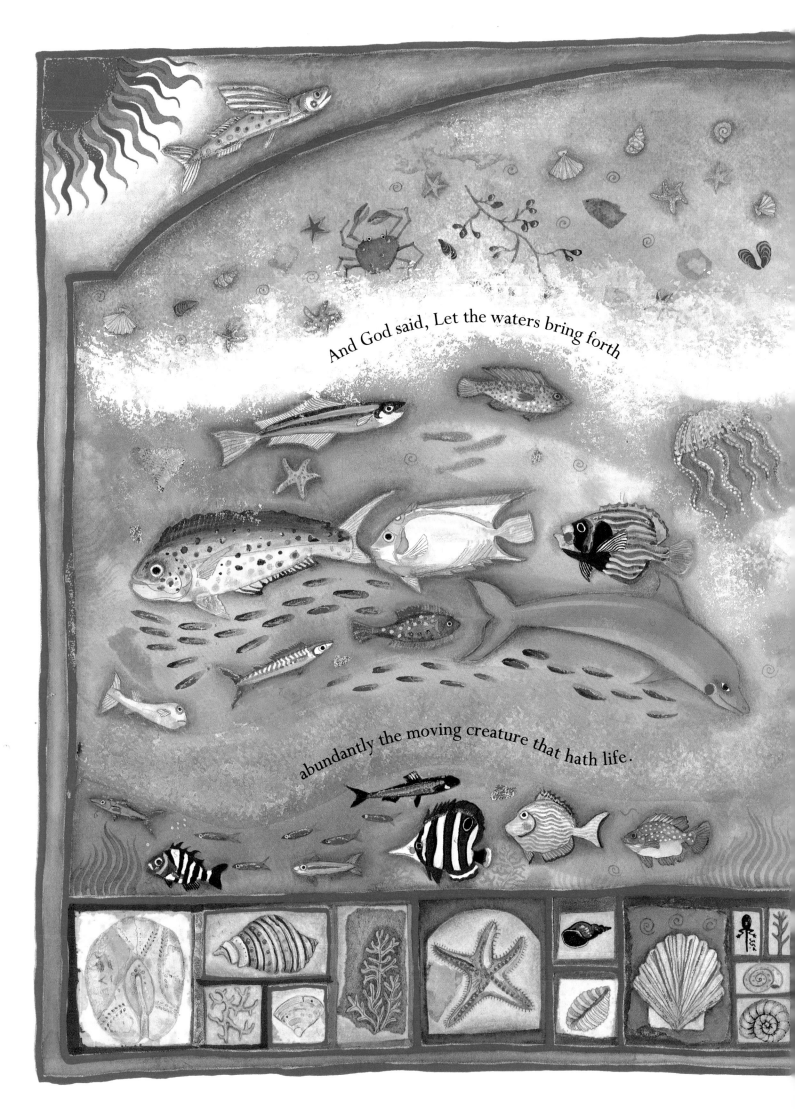

And God said, Let the waters bring forth

abundantly the moving creature that hath life.

And God created great whales, and every living creature that moveth, which the waters brought forth abundantly.

And God saw that it was good. And God blessed them, saying, Be fruitful, and multiply, and fill the waters in the seas.

And God said, Let there be fowl that may fly above the earth in the open
firmament of heaven.

And God created every winged fowl after its kind:

and God saw that it was good. And God blessed them,

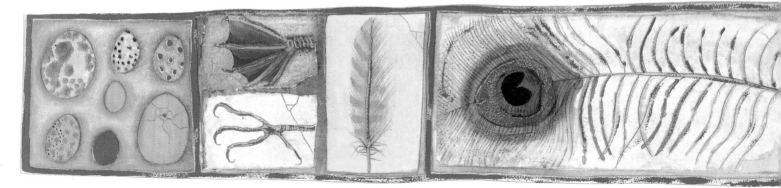

saying, Let fowl multiply in the earth.

And the evening and the morning were the fifth day.

And God said, Let the earth bring forth

the living creature after its kind,

cattle, and creeping thing, and beast of the earth: and it was so.

And God made the beast of the earth after its kind, and cattle after their kind, and every thing that creepeth upon the earth after its kind.

And God saw that it was good.

And God said, Let us make man and woman in our image, after our likeness: and let them have dominion over the fish of the sea, and over the fowl of the air, and over the cattle, and over all the earth, and over every creeping thing that creepeth upon the earth.

So God created humankind in his own image; male and female created
he them.

And God blessed them, and God said unto them, Be fruitful, and multiply, and replenish the earth: and have dominion over every living thing that moveth upon the earth.

And God saw every thing that he had made, and, behold, it was very good. And the evening and the morning were the sixth day.

Thus the heavens and the earth were finished, and all the host of them.
And on the seventh day God ended his work which he had made; and
he rested.

And that is a story of how the world began.

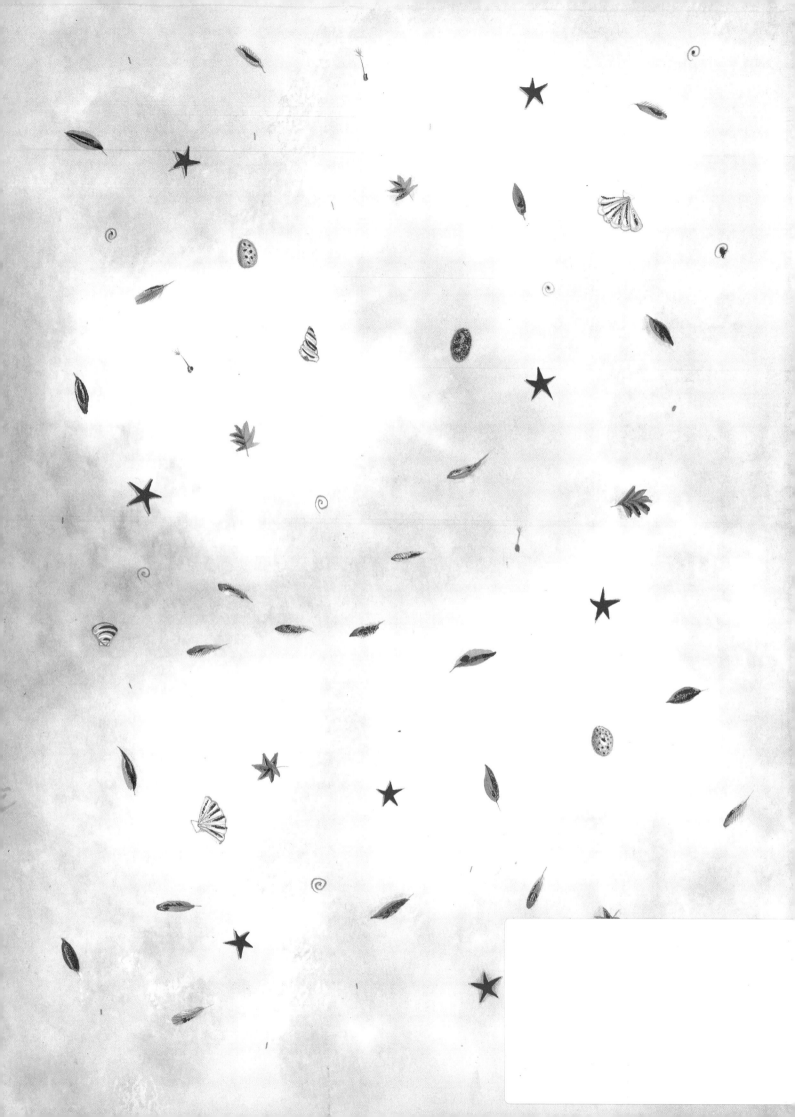